When I Come Up Missing

By
Cecelia Mallory

Copyright © 2011 by Cecelia Mallory

When I Come Up Missing
by Cecelia Mallory

Printed in the United States of America

ISBN 9781613791905

All rights reserved solely by the author. The author guarantees all contents are original and do not infringe upon the legal rights of any other person or work. No part of this book may be reproduced in any form without the permission of the author. The views expressed in this book are not necessarily those of the publisher.

Unless otherwise indicated, Bible quotations are taken from The NIV Version of the Bible. Copyright © 2005 by Zondervan.

www.xulonpress.com

Table of Contents

Introduction xi
1. The Annoying "Crazy" One 13
2. So What Is the Rapture and Why Should I Care? 19
3. The Rapture Has Come and Gone. Now What? 25
4. Eternal Life With Jesus or Eternal Life Without 33
   Prayer of Assurance 38
5. What Now? 41
6. Your Job and Your Future 43
7. I Always Love a Happy Ending! 49
Epilogue 51

Addendum.. 73
Question and Answer Session............. 111
Book and Website List......................... 119

Acknowledgements

This book would never have happened if it were not for the fact that God called my name and drew me unto Himself. For this I am forever grateful. The gift of forgiveness through Jesus' blood has allowed me to be transformed into a person He can use. Now the Holy Spirit is free to open my eyes to the Truth and counsel me as I apply the Word to my life. As I share with others the lessons that I am learning, I am so thankful that I have a purpose in Christ! I give all credit and acknowledgement to the Lord for this book and pray that only He will be glorified in it.

To my loving husband Kevin. Thank you for all of your encouragement and support and for helping me to see my usefulness for the Lord. Without you, life wouldn't be near as much fun!

Lastly, thank you Kelly, for helping me to reach my goals. Your editing has been greatly appreciated and your excitement has provided the energy I needed to keep moving forward.

Thanks to you all!

Author's Note

Throughout this booklet, I have provided Bible references to assist you in your understanding of this topic. The complete verses are listed in the addendum for your convenience. Also note that the verses listed are taken from the New International Version (NIV).

Introduction

I f you are reading this book, chances are a Christian gave it to you. It may have been a family member or a friend. It might have even been someone you barely know. No matter how it got into your hands, consider yourself blessed!

I wrote this book because I felt the need to prepare my family for my departure. Over the years I have shared the truths of the Bible with them and some weren't all that interested. This may be the case with you. And that's OK. This isn't a "get religion" book or an "I'm better than you" kind of thing. Consider it a Natural Disaster

Survival Guide. Because, believe me, if the events in this book occur in your lifetime, it will be the biggest disaster the non-Christian world has ever seen. Of course for the Christian, it won't be a disaster at all. It will be what we have all been waiting for: The Rapture.

By now I may have lost some of you but if you will agree to keep this book on your shelf, it may just be something that you pick up sometime down the road. In fact, it will be the FIRST book that you go to in the event that "I Come Up Missing".

1

The Annoying "Crazy" One

The person who gave this book to you has probably annoyed you at least once or twice, or even so much so that you finally said, "That's enough! If you want to come and visit, leave your religion at the door!" They talk about how Jesus died for your sins and that the only way to Heaven is to believe that fact. You might think, "I'm not perfect, but I am not a sinner." They say that there really is a hell and that YOU will be going there if you don't let Jesus be the Lord of your life. Well, no one is going to be Lord over you; that's why you live in America! Does any of this sound familiar? Maybe they even go so far as to say that loved ones who have passed are not in heaven even though they were "good"; or, the harder one to accept—that the "not-so-loved" ones may be there! Then they tell you that they care about you and that is why they share this with you.

Well you, my friend, are not alone. You are not the only one who has to put up with that annoying, crazy and delusional person. Some of my friends and family members feel the exact same way ... about me!

Until the late 1990's I was a normal, "living free and for myself" kind of person. I made my own choices and did my own thing, by golly. No one was going to instruct me on how to live or what to do with my life. My husband I and were struggling financially, had some pretty bad issues in our marriage and I was solving all of my problems with a food addiction. How's that for living free and for myself? A day came when I just couldn't take this freedom any longer. Because I had been raised in a "religious" family, I had been exposed to the Bible and little stories here and there about Jesus, but had no idea that I could have a personal relationship with Him. And, possibly like you, I just wasn't interested; until my life was in shambles. I realized that I couldn't fix the problems in my life so basically I decided to give God a try. It was a last resort. Well, low and behold, I started to change, my life started to improve and things were actually looking a little brighter! As time passed, day by day and year by year, not only did things improve, but I began to feel true freedom. It was amazing! Somewhere along the way, my husband started to notice the changes and he began to show an interest in what I was learning about God. It has now been about ten years since I began my journey with the Lord being in charge and my husband committed his ways to the Lord a few years after that. Our marriage is better than it has ever been, we are in a financial situation that is allowing us to bless others, and I am serving the Lord with everything I have in me. He is my Lord, my Savior and my King and I am no longer a slave in bondage to sin, debt or addiction; instead I have claimed my rightful place as a child of God Almighty, my Creator. This is how I became the annoying crazy one.

Although I may sound a little sarcastic in the presentation of this topic, it is a very serious one. If each of us is truly honest with ourselves, we would probably have to say that we have asked these questions at some point in our lives: Is there a Creator; what is my purpose here; and, is there something

When I Come Up Missing

after this life? All of these questions indicate a desire to know more about just the "here and now" and what we can visually see. God tells us in His Word that He has made Himself known to humankind and He provides us plenty of evidence to prove His existence. (Isaiah 11:9, Isaiah 44:24, Romans 1:18–20) So it would be natural that we would ask these questions at some point in our lives. I believe that in most cases we just don't really want the answers. If there is a God who has a purpose for each one of us and we do live beyond this life, then we are forced to face these truths and therefore will be required to make some very serious decisions. As I began to face these truths myself, I came to realize that this earthly life is just the tip of the iceberg. But because I had reached the end of myself, I was now willing to explore the answers to these questions. I have come to believe that the consequences of ignoring these truths are forever and irrevocable. It has become my life's goal to share with others what I have discovered and to prepare them for the decisions they will inevitably face some day. There will be no excuses for those who deny God's existence and His abundant love for us that was proven by Him offering His Son for our sins. I implore you to give this very serious contemplation and to courageously explore for yourself the answers to these universal questions of natural wonder. I believe that God placed in us a desire to know the truth so that as we seek the truth it will set us free just as He promised. John 8:31–32 says, "If you hold to my teaching, you are really my disciples. Then you will know the truth and the truth will set you free." (God has a lot to say about "truth" in His Word, so if you want to know more, find a concordance and look up all of the verses on this topic.)

2

So What Is the Rapture and Why Should I Care?

Hopefully by now I've got your attention and I encourage you to keep reading. It gets better or worse depending on how you look at it.

The crazy talk in Christian circles is that at some point and time in the future, and many think that it is in the near future, Jesus is coming back to collect His family. This includes all of the people who believe the Bible and call Jesus their Lord and savior. In an instant, in the blink of an eye, all true Christians on the face of the earth will vanish, just like that (1st Thessalonians 4:16–17). For some of you reading this, that day may be a dream come true: No more nagging conversations about God! In all seriousness, the truth is it will be the beginning of a very terrible time in history (Matthew 24:21). If you are still here after the Rapture, let me warn you, you will have wished that you had listened to your pesky friend.

Although the actual word "rapture" isn't found in the Bible, it was derived from the Latin word *raptus* used in the Latin vulgate or Bible. Raptus means to seize or transport. The original Greek word used was *harpazo*, which again means to snatch out or to seize. In 1st Thessalonians 4:17 the English phrase "caught up" is used, and therefore the word rapture has become the commonly used term for the return of the Lord for His family.

At first, the Rapture will cause tremendous chaos for those left behind. Very amazing and unusual things will occur during and immediately after the Rapture. People will vanish right before their eyes. Maybe they will be driving down the road and find themselves in a critical situation as cars become unpiloted, or coworkers will vanish while they are working. They may discover family members missing when they wake up, or the person sitting next to them on the bus or plane will disappear. It is believed that all children who are not old enough to make a decision for Christ will automatically be raptured. The world will be in chaos. There will be looting and rioting. The financial world will take a major dive because of fearful investors. The highways and byways will be blocked and congested with thousands and thousands of driverless vehicles. The airlines may not run for days if not weeks due to fear of another "episode" as well as lack of staff. Basically the world, but especially Christian nations, will shut down. Businesses and banks will close and grocery stores will be bare because trucks won't be running and people will be stocking up due to their fear. Imagine the absolute worst natural disaster and the affects that we would face and then double or triple that! It will be bad; very, very bad.

There will be all sorts of theories and ideas floating around about what happened. Many people may assume it was a massive alien abduction. So you don't believe in aliens either? To some, that theory will become more plausible than the return of Jesus for His family. Whatever the thoughts and misconstrued ideas, it will be a mystery. To keep peace and to calm the citizens, the rulers of the world will have some creative lies concocted that will keep people content. And, we are not talking about a few thousand people coming up missing. We are talking MILLIONS! It will be the greatest loss of life in history. I use the word loss because to those left behind it will be, but to those missing, it will be the greatest blessing imaginable.

3

The Rapture Has Come and Gone. Now What?

After the chaos of the Rapture subsides things will begin to look better. There will be a man who steps up to the plate to help organize things and calm the world's fears. He will make everyone feel much better and will seem like, oh I don't know ... a messiah? Oh, that's right, you don't believe in the need for a savior. You may by this time. But don't be fooled! He is a wolf in sheep's clothing!

When I Come Up Missing

This is where it starts to get seriously scary for those who are not raptured.

The Rapture will be the start of a new era on earth. Most Christians believe that it will signify the beginning of what is called the Tribulation period, a seven year period of time when major changes will take place, from political to spiritual. It is best described as the beginning of the end. The Bible gives us much detail about the events that will take place during this time. The book of Revelation is God's warning to us and tells us about this future time. Chapters 6–19 of Revelation detail the wrath of God that will be poured out during the Tribulation. There is even a series of books that you may be familiar with called *Left Behind*. Even though the characters and some of the specific details are fictional, the series is based on biblical prophecy, and the first book of the series begins just a few minutes before the Rapture occurs.

Many of the events believed will occur during the Tribulation include an eventual one-world government, one-world religion and one-world currency just to name a few. These three alone cause shivers to run down my spine. And even though the idea of these things occurring seems remote, I suggest that you take a look at the current events happening not only in our country, but around the world. The things that will take place in the early part of the Tribulation are already starting to develop as I write this book. In order for the events described in God's Word to come about, there needs to be a certain amount of deterioration within the world beforehand. We are seeing that right now. Natural disasters are happening globally at an unusual rate. Many have been record breaking, like Katrina, the tsunami in Sri Lanka, the recent flooding in Pakistan and the list goes on. The political system in America is in crisis and the people are fed up. The financial system worldwide is strained and in some places truly failing, like Greece and the state of California. The tensions in the Middle East and over Israel are escalating at a staggering rate. All of these things are setting the stage for the perfect situation in which biblical prophecy can be fulfilled when the Rapture occurs. So even though a world government isn't currently on the menu, the main ingredients are being stirred together and all that is needed now is an overwhelming crisis to turn up the heat! Aren't you the least bit interested or curious yet?

Now, this man who has come to save the day will bring world peace, or so it will seem. He will be placed in a position of high authority and at some point will become the leader of world; a one-world government. He will have charisma and charm and will even get Israel and Palestine to come to terms and agree to rebuild the temple in Jerusalem. All will seem rosy. But don't give into his façade. He is really the anti-Christ!! Yep, there's that word that only wacko Christians use and believe in. This is what God tells us in the book of Daniel regarding the anti-Christ: "The king will do as he pleases. He will exalt and magnify himself above every god and will say unheard of things against the God of gods. He will be successful until the time of wrath is completed, for what has been determined must take place" (Daniel 11:36).

Well, right now (assuming the Rapture has NOT yet occurred) you may be thinking that this fictional book is truly a waste of your time. Yet, you might possibly be intrigued enough to see how it all ends. If the Rapture has happened, you are amazed at the accuracy of the events and how they have unfolded before your very eyes. Read on ...

Mr. Anti-Christ (Mr. A-C) will be doing great. He will be making everyone happy and giving people exactly what they think they need. The world will appear to be coming together in ways that was never thought possible. So the need for God and the time for prayer will have passed. (I am assuming here that this is what everyone will try immediately following the Rapture. In fact many will probably believe that Mr. A-C is an answer to prayer! WRONG!) This very false sense of security will last for three and one-half years; long enough to get most people on board with his way of thinking. There will be a one-world religion, one currency, and the one-world government run by yours truly "Mr. A-C". Have you ever heard of the mark of the beast; that myth or crazy notion that there will be a mark on your hand if you belong to the devil? Well, my friend, guess what? It isn't fiction any longer. In order to buy food, get fuel or get medical care you will need to have some kind of permanent identification (Revelation 13:11–17). And I mean permanent! It may be an implanted bar code or a brand of some sort. I vote for the bar code—it would be much less painful. Since I am going to be in heaven with Jesus, though, I guess it doesn't matter what option I would choose! And in order to get this privileged mark, you will have to deny that Jesus is the Son of God! How about that? Do you know what that really means?

4

Everlasting Life With Jesus or Everlasting Life Without

Do you know that no matter what other world religions say, you DO live forever? Yep, that's right. It's all right there in black, white and red. God says in the Bible, that we will live forever (Matthew 25:46). Doesn't that sound great?

So, back to the previous question of denying Jesus; maybe you are saying, "So what?" of course I would deny Him if it meant food, fuel or my health. Many of you may be saying that it doesn't matter if any of those things are at stake, you would deny Him anyhow. In fact, you have been up until now if you are not a true Christian. This is where things take a very critical turn. You are faced with a choice and that is the whole goal of this book: to help you prepare for that decision.

If you have already experienced the Rapture, this choice will hopefully be an easy one. We'll talk in a minute, but if the world has not gone through the events that are outlined here, listen up.

God says in His Word, the Bible, that there is a heaven and a hell. Everlasting life means that you live in one of the two places. To qualify for heaven you need to completely understand and believe that you are born a sinner and are in need of a Savior; Jesus, who is that Savior, is fully God and fully man; and, He came to earth and died for YOUR sins, was resurrected and is now seated in heaven. (John 3:16–18) That's it! No trying to be perfect, because you can't. No doing "good" works to "work" your way in. Nope, none of those things earn you a thing in regards to getting in. Yep, it is that simple. The other option is to deny these truths. If you choose to disagree with even one of them then unfortunately the news isn't as good. Hell is where you will be going. FOREVER! This, by the way, is a really long time. I know, you don't believe in hell. That's OK, because you don't have to believe in it for it to be real. You can deny its existence all that you want, but if you deny Jesus, you'll get to experience first-hand what hell is like. From the description that God gives us in His Word, it will be worse than a person could imagine (Matthew 13:42, 49–50). Think of it this way: Hell = the absence of God, and God = everything good. You do the math.

Still not sold on this whole rapture and heaven thing? Well, it truly is my prayer that everyone who reads this book will contemplate these things and keep this book even if you don't believe it. It is my great hope that you would listen to the one who gave it to you, that you would at least seek out answers to the many questions that I know you have but are nervous to ask. I have been where you are and there are many questions that can cause a person who doesn't know God, to doubt Him and His Word. Things that come to my mind are: How can you trust the Bible to be true after so many translations or even because of the fact that it was written by man? How can good people go to hell? Why does God allow suffering? What I would encourage you to do is to engage the person who gave you this book, in a debate of sorts. If they don't have the answers ask them to find them for you. I am pretty certain they will be happy to do that. I have provided a Q and A session in the back to help stimulate a conversation. I cannot make it clear enough how important a relationship with God is to each and every person on the face of this earth. A "final answer" will be required before you take your last breath and the choice you make will be a non-revocable one. I would hate to think that you made the wrong one. God says in His Word, that He wants **no one** to perish (2nd Peter 3:9). Maybe you would ask why He doesn't let everyone into heaven if He doesn't want anyone to perish. This is a fair question and the answer is really quite simplistic; it's called free will. We are given the choice to choose heaven and as I mentioned before, the requirement is simply believing God and His Word.

So, if you are reading this book and your Christian friends are still walking the earth, you are blessed to still have time. Talk to God and accept the gift of forgiveness and everlasting life in heaven before He comes for His Family. On the other hand, if the Rapture has occurred already, please, KEEP READING!

Below is a prayer that you can pray if you are ready to turn your life over to God. Make it personal and from the heart and God will hear your prayer. If you have read enough to believe, you are heaven bound!

Pray:
Jesus, God, creator of all, I come before you with a heart that is ready to accept you. I realize that I am a sinner; that I can't be good enough on my own to be with you forever, but that through the gift of Your Son, Jesus, who died on the cross for me, I can have a personal relationship with you and have eternal life with you in heaven. Lord

Jesus, forgive me for my sins and come into my life and guide me. Give me strength to face the coming trials and the strength to share your Truth with others. I pray these things in the name of Jesus. Amen.

Praise the Lord!! You will be eternally with Jesus and the rest of His family!

5

What Now?

If you are still reading this and have prayed the previous prayer, you need to know what to do next. So whether or not the Rapture has occurred, you can rest easy. God is now in control of your life and whatever happens from here on out, He will give you the strength to continue to trust Him. Find a Bible and start reading it. There are also some books and authors listed in the back that will help you to develop your relationship with the Lord as well as some websites that are biblical and trustworthy.

When I Come Up Missing

Set aside time each day to talk to Jesus and to read His Word. Prayer can be a very intimidating thing, but just talk to God like you would your best friend. Tell Him how you are feeling and what you need (e.g., strength, courage, wisdom, provisions, protection etc.). The Bible says that the Holy Spirit prays on our behalf when we don't know what to pray (Romans 8:26) so you can rely on your Counselor (John 14:16–17) to give you a hand. And, don't forget to thank Him (Philippians 4:6–7)!

6

Your Job and Your Future

Before the Rapture or after, the job of the Christian is to show God's love to others and to share with them His Word. So no matter what your daily life looks like, do these things. The reading list offers some help in this area, and as you seek God's direction He will show you what He has for you as an individual.

Moving on, we look at a world after the Rapture and what it will be like for those who have accepted the Lord during this time.

Now comes the hard part. Because you have chosen the side of God, Satan is mad. He really isn't too happy that you have walked off of his team. So get prepared for some hard times. (This is true even for those who come to the Lord before the Rapture.)

God says in His Word that His wrath will be unleashed during the Tribulation (Revelation 14:10) and Satan will be hanging on for dear life. You will face times like no other times (Matthew 24:15–28), but God will be with you through His Holy Spirit. He will guide you and protect you until your job on earth is done. Some of you may make it through the Tribulation and some of you won't, but until God takes you out of the game your job will be to share with others the Truth of His Word. As I mentioned earlier, God says that He doesn't want anyone to perish, so He will help you to get His Word to as many people as will listen. This won't be easy, but the rewards will be beyond your imagination. It is believed that more people will come to trust in Jesus during the Tribulation than during any other time in history! But, more people will die for Him during that time than ever before. I suggest that you give this some serious thought!

The last three and one-half years of the Tribulation will probably be worse than anyone could even describe. God tells us that Mr. A-C will reveal his true nature and will require people to bow down to him. He will think nothing of killing those who don't and will make Hitler look like an angel. At the end of the Tribulation, the "Day of the Lord" will occur which is also known as Armageddon (Revelation 19:11–21). On this day, Jesus will return to earth and defeat Satan. During the Tribulation, Mr. A-C will have taken complete control of the world and it will become a war of good vs. evil. Satan, being the big loser, will be cast into hell for the next 1,000 years (Revelation 20:2). This period of time is called the Millennial Reign or Millennial Kingdom. Jesus will be reigning on earth from Jerusalem and all of His family who died from the beginning of time will return with Him to help Him reign (Revelation 20:4). It is during this time, that the people who came to trust in Jesus during the Tribulation and are still alive will repopulate the earth. For 1,000 years there will be no influence of Satan and sin. BUT, "free will" will still exist, and toward the end of the Millennial Reign, Jesus will release Satan long enough for people born during this time to express their free will and choose God or Satan (Revelation 20:7). I used to think that without Satan's influence, people would naturally choose God, but sin has been a part of our nature since the "fall" of Adam and Eve. So there will be people who choose to deny Jesus even though He will be present and reigning on earth.

All of this culminates with the Great White Throne Judgment where Jesus once and for all casts Satan and his followers into the Lake of Fire, forever (Revelation 20:10). There will be a new heaven and a new earth (Revelation 21:1) and peace will reign for eternity (Revelation 22:3–5). The End.

7

I Always Love a Happy Ending!

So, there you have it! For me and the one who gave you this book, it is a happy ending. And, hopefully it has become one for you, too, by your trust in the Lord Jesus Christ, but if you are still not sure or think that Christians are a little off their rocker, PLEASE remember where you stashed this book in the event that "I Come Up Missing"!

"Behold, I am coming soon! Blessed is he who keeps the words of the prophecy in this book." Revelation 22:7

Epilogue

The following is something that I put together in case you are interested in understanding the Bible a little better. It is brief but may answer some of the questions that you have. The Addendum contains most of the verses that I have listed and I encourage you to read them. If a Bible is available to you, I would suggest that you look them up as you read through the Epilogue to become more acquainted with where things are in His Word.

I couldn't possible give a complete outline of the Bible in this brief amount of space, so I went where I felt the Lord was

leading me. There are awesome stories that I didn't include, but I hope that I did include enough to get you interested and to cause you to want to know more.
So let's begin ...

What is the Bible? Well, it isn't a book full of laws and commandments and it isn't full of God's wrath and holy wars, like many believe. What it is, is a story, from beginning to end: The story of God's creation (you and I), His love for us and the plan that He had from the beginning of time to share eternity with us.

As you follow the Bible references listed here they will take you on a journey of understanding. They will show you step by step His plan for you and that of mankind's. If you are willing to open your mind and your heart, be prepared to experience a journey like never before.

- For proof of the existence of God read Genesis 1:1, Isaiah 40:26 and Romans 1:20. The Romans passage says that we have no excuse but to know that He exists through His creations.
- If you believe that He exists but don't believe the Bible is true or accurate check out: 2nd Timothy 3:16, Psalm 111:7–8, Psalm 119:160, Revelation 22:18–19, 2nd Peter 1:21 and Hebrews 4:12.
- Why should we read the Bible? I can't say it any better than God Himself did in the following verses: 2nd Timothy 3:16–17, Psalm 119:105, Romans 10:17, John 8:31–32, 1st Peter 2:2, Jeremiah 15:16 and Colossians 1:25–27.

Do you want to know more? Let's take a quick trip through God's Word together.

When I Come Up Missing

Don't take my word for the facts you are about to read; dig deep into God's Word to verify these facts and to uncover even more about the things I mention here.

"Now the Bereans were of more noble character than the Thessalonians, for they received the message with great eagerness and examined the Scriptures every day to see if what Paul said was true." Acts 17:11

Bible Basics 101

The Bible is comprised of 66 different books written by over 40 different authors (all of which is inspired by God; see 2nd Timothy 3:16). The first book is Genesis and covers from the beginning of creation, through the story of Noah and ends with the life of Joseph. It's filled with great stories—you should read it sometime! In fact, how much do you know about Adam and

Eve? Their story is about more than an apple. Briefly, God's original intent was for His creation, us—mankind, to spend eternity with Him in Paradise. But we messed that up when Adam and Eve doubted God and trusted the serpent by eating from the tree of knowledge of good and evil. By the way, the Bible didn't say it was an apple! So He had to banish them from Paradise, the Garden of Eden (Genesis 3:23). Because God is perfect and holy He cannot tolerate sin (Hebrews 7:26). Disobedience is sin and Adam and Eve brought upon the entire existence of mankind, the wage or payment for sin, which is death (Romans 6:23). We are talking about not only physical death but spiritual death or separation from God. But, God was not surprised by their disobedience nor is He surprised by ours. He had a plan so that we could still spend eternity with Him in heaven. Intrigued? Read on!

Most people have heard about Noah and his ark. Yes, just like the Adam and Eve "apple" story, his is about more than just an ark. Prior to the ark, man had become corrupt (Genesis 6:11–14). All but Noah and his family, that is. Noah was a righteous man. Anyhow, God wanted to save Noah but planned to destroy the rest of mankind. He was fed up with our wicked and corrupt ways. So God told Noah to build and ark. This was not a weekend project. It took him 120 years. (Yes, people did live to be 800–900 years old during this time. Read the family tree of Adam in Genesis chapter 5.) Now, the interesting part of this is that God could have destroyed all of mankind and saved Noah in the blink of an eye, right? But He didn't. Why? Well, to give the rest of humanity a chance to turn to Him. He really does not want us to perish (2nd Peter 3:9). Unfortunately no one did and Noah and his family were the only survivors. Remember this story when we talk about Jesus.

Another very interesting story is about Abraham and Sarah. He and Sarah had no children and they were getting old, way beyond the childbearing age when God told him that he would have a son. Well, ten years went by without a pregnancy and Abraham began to wonder if maybe he had misunderstood God. So Sarah suggested that they use a surrogate for the child. Hagar, Sarah's maidservant became pregnant with Abraham's child. This however was not God's plan. In God's timing Sarah did become pregnant with Isaac. It was typical in those days for the firstborn son to receive the blessing from the father so Hagar may have expected Ishmael to receive Abraham's blessing. Although in this case, it was God's plan for Isaac to be the blessed descendant. This is another good illustration that God will bless His plans for our lives, but if we choose to make things happen, we can usually expect to be disappointed. The interesting point to this story is that Isaac became the father of Judaism and ultimately Christian religions and Ishmael the father of Islam. The fight over the blessing goes on to this day!

There are many other good stories in Genesis such as the trickery that Jacob pulled on his brother Essau and later the trickery that was pulled on him, the life of Joseph and how his brothers sold him into slavery yet in the end he saved them from famine. The list goes on and so must I, so just go read it!

The next 4 books; Exodus, Leviticus, Numbers and Deuteronomy all have to do with Moses and his call from God to rescue the Israelites from Egypt. Israel's foundations for truly becoming a nation and God's chosen people began here.

Many people are familiar with the Ten Commandments themselves as well as the movie classic of the same name. Although not completely accurate, it does a fair job of depicting the life of Moses. However, many important stories are not covered in the movie. Even though we get a decent picture of the man Moses, we don't see the full picture that God was painting. Did you know that the journey from the Red Sea to the "Promised Land" was only a couple weeks of travel at best? How long did they wander the desert? 40 years! Why? Well, they were stubborn and didn't trust God. This is exactly why many of us seem to wander through life without knowing that we are just outside our Promised Land if we would only trust Jesus! Hmm. Interesting! How about the whole bout of plagues; do you remember the last one where the Pharaoh's son dies as does the first born of all of Egypt? The Bible tells us of the specific instructions that God gave the Israelites to be saved from this plague. They were to choose a lamb from the flock that was a firstborn without blemish. They were to bring it in to their house for a couple of days prior to the night of the plague. On that night they were to slaughter it and place its blood on the doorposts of their house so that the angel of death would "pass over" their home and save the firstborn of their families from death. Without the blood on the door, indicating their faith in God's plan to save them, they would lose their firstborn child. WOW! That kind of sounds like the claim that Christians make about Jesus and the fact that if we put our faith in Him and believe that His blood will remove our iniquities, we will be saved from spiritual death also known as hell.

Another fact that isn't covered at all in the movie is the thousands of animal sacrifices that were performed to cover the Israelites sins. Even with the Ten Commandments and the additional laws that God gave to the Israelites, they were unable to remain an obedient, holy and righteous people. This was another key that pointed to the need for Jesus. If God's chosen people couldn't be good enough to enter God's kingdom of eternal life, then who would be? No one, without God's help! (Romans 3:10–12) God used the nation of Israel to prove to them as well as the rest of the world, the need for a perfect sacrifice that wouldn't just **cover** the sin of mankind, but **remove** it! All of these events are in the book of Exodus if your interest has been peaked.

The remainder of the Old Testament covers the history of Israel and Judah, as well as some stories about individuals like Esther, Ruth, and Job. It has songs in the book of Psalms, wise thoughts in Proverbs, and covers very important prophecies, past and future, throughout the books written by prophets like Daniel, Isaiah, and Ezekiel. If you had only the Old Testament available to you, like the Jews did in the BC years, you'd be waiting on the edge of your seat. The Old Testament points not only to the need of a savior, but it tells of the promise from God to send one!

This is where the New Testament picks up: The birth of our Lord and Savior, Jesus Christ. I have heard it put this way: The Old Testament describes the Law and God's Promise, and the New Testament fulfills them both through Jesus' life, death, and resurrection.

Matthew, Mark, Luke, and John record His life, ministry, teachings, crucifixion, and death. They also record His resurrection and ascension into heaven. They give proofs of His deity (John 1:1–3) and the truth that He is the only way for us to receive grace from God and the gift of eternal life in heaven (John 14:6). They record when John the Baptist exclaimed, "Look, the Lamb of God who takes away the sin of the world" (John 1:29). (NOTE: This statement alone summarizes the points made previously about the slaughtered lamb's blood of Passover and the blood of the sacrifices made in the Old Testament pointing to Jesus.) They record the words from Jesus Himself and the promise to those who believe in Him of the gift of a helper/counselor called the Holy Spirit (John 14:16–17). These four books are packed with insight into how to live in a way that is pleasing to

God. They show us that Jesus is our source of rest (Matthew 11:28–30) and our rock (Matthew 7:24–27). They record numerous miracles to help confirm His power and authority over all things. Ultimately, they record His resurrection, which is the foundation of Christian faith. He IS alive and seated at the right hand of the Father in heaven, right now!

The book of Acts kicks off the true beginning of the church. Not churches like Catholic or Baptist churches but the **body** of people who believed then and now that Jesus was and is the Christ. It is filled with the transformation of lives like Saul who, being a devout Jew tormented and killed numerous Christians. But, one day, on his way to Damascus, Jesus spoke to him in a blinding light (Acts 9:1–9). It was an amazing transformation from unbelief into belief in the blink of an eye. Saul, renamed

When I Come Up Missing

Paul, goes on to be one of the greatest disciples for Christ's work, which is sharing the gospel or "good news" of Jesus with others. Acts records his missionary journeys and the numerous miracles that God performed to help Paul do His work. It is one of my favorite books. It also tells of the work that Peter and many of the other disciples did. Sadly, it records some of the persecution and as a result some of their deaths for the sake of Jesus. Sad for us, but glorious for them; they are in heaven with Jesus!

The next section of books is actually letters written to different churches (bodies of believers) like Corinth (1st & 2nd Corinthians) and Philippi (Philippians) as well as to individuals like Timothy and Philemon. These were all written by Paul (Hebrews is believed to have been written by Paul, but it is not certain). On his missionary journeys through Asia Minor and into Rome, he taught groups of people who came to believe in Jesus. These groups were the beginning of the first churches, so the letters that he wrote were sometimes to encourage them and sometimes to rebuke them for various behaviors. These letters are full of insight and depth. They offer wisdom and direction for living a life of joy and blessing. They give instruction for handling difficult times and persecution. They are truly amazing. Take one per month and read them thoroughly. You will be blessed.

The books of James, 1st and 2nd Peter, 1st, 2nd and 3rd John, and Jude were written by James, Peter, John, and Jude. They, too, are letters, more like memoirs. The authors share their insight and love of Jesus. They encourage and teach believers to show their faith by their actions (James). They give warnings of false teachers (2nd Peter and 1st John) and even teach about how wives and husbands should treat each other (1st Peter).

The next paragraph looks like a rabbit trail but bear with me.

Why the Bible is being removed from our daily lives and is being denied access to our children is beyond me! It is the best textbook available for teaching mankind how to live in a way that not only pleases God, but will bless us in the end! Who doesn't want to have done unto them what another person would? You know the golden rule? Where did it come from? Matthew 7:12. It was spoken directly from the mouth of Jesus, God Himself! In addition, God says in Deuteronomy 6:1–9 that the greatest commandment of all is to love the Lord your God with all of your heart, with all of your soul and with all of your strength. He goes on to say that these words shall live in our hearts, we shall teach them diligently to our children, and we are to talk of them when we are sitting in our houses (TURN OFF THAT TV!), walking and even lying down. He even states that we shall write them on our doorposts and gates. So why are His Words being removed from everything and why are they the last thing that we talk about anymore? Better yet, most people cringe when we talk about the Bible or use the word God unless we are swearing, then it is OK. What has changed over the years and why is it so backwards? Well, God tells us in Romans 1:18–2:9. It completely describes the state of mankind today.

The last book of the Bible is called Revelation. It is the recorded revelation that God gave to John, the same writer of John the gospel and 1st–3rd John. He was exiled to an island called Patmos after they tried killing him by dipping him in a vat of boiling oil. God is so good; it didn't work and God blessed him with the prophetic revelation of Jesus Christ and the end of the story. The book of Revelation is the last piece of the puzzle and is packed with future prophecies. Not only does it describe our future but it is the end of the story of God's perfect plan for renewal. It is the answer to all of the turmoil and confusion that we see today.

Do you remember when we talked about Noah and the ark? I suggested that you remember the story when we talked about Jesus. Well, we have been living in a grace period. That period of time it took for Noah to build the ark offered 120 years for people to turn to God. They didn't. Since the birth of Christ, we have been given the opportunity to turn to God. Have you? Are you going to perish when God has had enough? Or are you going to jump aboard the "ark"

When I Come Up Missing

of Jesus to be saved? It is your choice. That is where free will comes in. God could MAKE you choose, but He doesn't. But, He does give you plenty of time and opportunity to choose Him on your own. Which will it be for you? Those who were around in Noah's time must have thought that he was a little cuckoo. Well, too bad for them. Do you think that your Christian friends and family members are cuckoo as well? Maybe you just call them a little over the top. It doesn't seem so harsh that way. It doesn't matter. You are not really denying them and their faith; you are denying God and His love for you. Believing in God isn't enough, even the devil and his demons believe in God and tremble, but they are still going to spend eternity in hell (James 2:19).

Believe in this and you shall be saved:

"For God so loved the world that He gave His one and only Son, that whoever believes in Him shall not perish but have eternal life. For God did not send His Son into the world to condemn the world, but to save the world through Him. Whoever believes in Him is not condemned, but whoever does not believe stands condemned already because he has not believed in the name of God's one and only Son." John 3:16–18

Addendum

Chapter 1

- Isaiah 11:9
  - "… for the earth will be full of the knowledge of the Lord…"
- Isaiah 44:24
  - "This is what the Lord says—your Redeemer who formed you in the womb: I am the Lord who has made all things, who alone stretched out the heavens, who spread out the earth by Myself."

- Romans 1:19–20
  - "since what may be know about God is plain to them, because God has made it plain to them. For since the creation of the world God's invisible qualities—His eternal power and divine nature—have been clearly seen, being understood from what has been made, so that men are without excuse."

Chapter 2

- 1st Thessalonians 4:16–17
  - "For the Lord himself will come down from heaven, with a loud command, with the voice of the archangel and with the trumpet call of God, and the dead in Christ will rise first. After that, we who are still

alive and are left will be caught up together with them in the clouds to meet the Lord in the air. And so we will be with the Lord forever."

- Matthew 24:21
  - "For then there will be great distress, unequaled from the beginning of the world until now—and never to be equaled again."

Chapter 3

- Revelation 13:11–17
  - "Then I saw another beast, coming out of the earth. He had two horns like a lamb, but he spoke like a dragon. He exercised all the authority of the first beast on his behalf, and made the earth and its

inhabitants worship the first beast, whose fatal wound had been healed. And he performed great and miraculous signs, even causing fire to come down from heaven to earth in full view of men. Because of the signs he was given power to do on behalf of the first beast, he deceived the inhabitants of the earth. He ordered them to set up an image in honor of the beast who was wounded by the sword and yet lived. He was given power to give breath to the image of the first beast, so that it could speak and cause all who refused to worship the image to be killed. He also forced everyone, small and great, rich and poor, free and slave, to receive a mark on his right hand or on his forehead, so that no one could buy or sell unless he had the mark, which is the name of the beast or the number of his name."

Chapter 4

- ♦ Matthew 25:46
  - o "Then they will go away to eternal punishment, but the righteous to eternal life."
- ♦ John 3:16–18
  - o "For God so loved the world that he gave his one and only Son, that whoever believes in him shall not perish but have eternal life. For God did not send his Son into the world to condemn the world, but to save the world through him.

Whoever believes in him is not condemned, but whoever does not believe stands condemned already because he has not believed in the name of God's one and only Son."

- Matthew 13:42, 49–50
    - "They will throw them into the fiery furnace, where there will be weeping and gnashing of teeth."
    - "This is how it will be at the end of the age. The angels will come and separate the wicked from the righteous and throw them into the fiery furnace, where there will be weeping and gnashing of teeth."
- 2nd Peter 3:9
    - "The Lord is not slow in keeping his promise, as some under-

stand slowness. He is patient with you, not wanting anyone to perish, but everyone to come to repentance."

Chapter 5

- Romans 8:26
  - "In the same way, the Spirit helps us in our weakness. We do not know what we ought to pray for, but the Spirit himself intercedes for us with groans that words cannot express."
- John 14:16–17
  - "And I will ask the Father, and he will give you another Counselor to be with you forever—the Spirit of truth. The world cannot accept him, because it neither sees him nor knows him. But you know

him, for he lives with you and will be in you."

- Philippians 4:6–7
  - "Do not be anxious about anything, but in everything, by prayer and petition, with thanksgiving, present your requests to God. And the peace of God, which transcends all understanding, will guard your hearts and your minds in Christ Jesus."

Chapter 6

- Revelation 14:10
  - "he too, will drink of the wine of God's fury, which has been poured full strength into the cup of his wrath. He will be tormented with burning sulfur in

the presence of the holy angels and of the Lamb."

- Matthew 24:15–28
  - "So when you see standing in the holy place 'the abomination that causes desolation,' spoken of through the prophet Daniel—let the reader understand—then let those who are in Judea flee to the mountains. Let no one on the roof of his house go down to take anything out of the house. Let no one in the field go back to get his cloak. How dreadful it will be in those days for pregnant women and nursing mothers! Pray that your flight will not take place in winter or on the Sabbath. For then there will be great distress, unequaled from

the beginning of the world until now—and never to be equaled again. If those days had not been cut short, no one would survive, but for the sake of the elect those days will be shortened. At that time if anyone says to you, 'Look, here is the Christ!' or, 'There he is!' do not believe it. For false Christs and false prophets will appear and perform great signs and miracles to deceive even the elect—if that were possible. See, I have told you ahead of time. So if anyone tells you, 'There he is, out in the desert,' do not go out; or, 'Here he is, in the inner rooms,' do not believe it. For as lightning that comes from the east is visible even in the west, so will be the coming of the Son of Man. Wherever there is a carcass, there the vultures will gather."

- Revelation 19:11–21
  - "I saw heaven standing open and there before me was a white horse, whose rider is called Faithful and True. With justice he judges and makes war. His eyes are like blazing fire, and on his head are many crowns. He has a name written on him that no one knows but he himself. He is dressed in a robe dipped in blood, and his name is the Word of God. The armies of heaven were following him, riding on white horses and dressed in fine linen, white and clean. Out of his mouth comes

a sharp sword with which to strike down the nations. "He will rule them with an iron scepter." He treads the winepress of the fury of the wrath of God Almighty. On his robe and on his thigh he has this name written: KING OF KINGS AND LORD OF LORDS. And I saw an angel standing in the sun, who cried in a loud voice to all the birds flying in midair, "Come, gather together for the great supper of God, so that you may eat the flesh of kings, generals, and mighty men, of horses and their riders, and the flesh of all people, free and slave, small and great." Then I saw the beast and the kings of the earth and their armies gathered together to make war against the rider on the horse and his army. But the beast was captured, and with him the false prophet who had performed the miraculous signs on his behalf. With these signs he had deluded those who had received the mark of the beast and worshiped his image. The two of them were thrown alive into the fiery lake of burning sulfur. The rest of them were killed with the sword that came out of the mouth of the rider on the horse, and all the birds gorged themselves on their flesh."

- Revelation 20:2
  - "He seized the dragon, that ancient serpent, who is the

devil, or Satan, and bound him for a thousand years."

- Revelation 20:4
  - "I saw thrones on which were seated those who had been given authority to judge. And I saw the souls of those who had been beheaded because of their testimony for Jesus and because of the word of God. They had not worshiped the beast or his image and had not received his mark on their foreheads or their hands. They came to life and reigned with Christ a thousand years."
- Revelation 20:7
  - "When the thousand years are over, Satan will be released from his prison"

- Revelation 20:10
  - "And the devil, who deceived them, was thrown into the lake of burning sulfur, where the beast and the false prophet had been thrown. They will be tormented day and night forever and ever."
- Revelation 21:1
  - "Then I saw a new heaven and a new earth, for the first heaven and the first earth had passed away, and there was no longer any sea."
- Revelation 22:3–5
  - "No longer will there be any curse. The throne of God and of the Lamb will be in the city, and his servants will serve him. They will see his face, and his name will be on their fore-

heads. There will be no more night. They will not need the light of a lamp or the light of the sun, for the Lord God will give them light. And they will reign forever and ever."

Epilogue

- Genesis 1:1
    - "In the beginning God created the heavens and the earth."
- Isaiah 40:26
    - "Lift your eyes and look to the heavens: Who created all these? He who brings out the starry host one by one, and calls them each by name. Because of his great power and mighty strength, not one of them is missing."

- Romans 1:20
    - "For since the creation of the world God's invisible qualities—His eternal power and divine nature—have been clearly seen, being understood from what has been made. So that men are without excuse."
- 2nd Timothy 3:16
    - "All Scripture is God-breathed and is useful for teaching, rebuking, correcting and training in righteousness"
- Psalm 111:7–8
    - "The works of His hands are faithful and just; all His precepts are trustworthy. They are steadfast forever and ever, done in faithfulness and uprightness."

- Psalm 119:160
    - "All Your words are true; all Your righteous laws are eternal."
- Revelation 22:18–19
    - "I warn everyone who hears the words of the prophesy of this book: If anyone adds anything to them, God will add to him the plagues described in this book. And if anyone takes words away from this book of prophesy, God will take away from him his share in the tree of life and in the holy city, which are described in this book."
- 2nd Peter 1:21
    - "For prophesy never had its origin in the will of man, but men spoke from God as they

were carried along by the Holy Spirit."

- Hebrews 4:12
  - "For the Word of God is living and active. Sharper than any double-edged sword, it penetrates even to dividing soul and spirit, joints and marrow; it judges the thoughts and attitudes of the heart."
- 2nd Timothy 3:16–17
  - "All Scripture is God-breathed and is useful for teaching, rebuking, correcting and training in righteousness, so that the man of God may be thoroughly equipped for every good work."
- Psalm 119:105
  - "Your word is a lamp to my feet and a light for my path."

- Romans 10:17
    - "Consequently, faith comes from hearing the message, and the message is heard through the word of Christ."
- John 8:31–32
    - "To the Jews who had believed him, Jesus said, "If you hold to my teaching, you are really my disciples. Then you will know the truth, and the truth will set you free."
- 1st Peter 2:2
    - "Like newborn babies, crave pure spiritual milk, so that by it you may grow up in your salvation"
- Jeremiah 15:16
    - "When your words came, I ate them; they were my joy and my

heart's delight, for I bear your name, O LORD God Almighty."

- ◆ Colossians 1:25–27
    - o "I have become its servant by the commission God gave me to present to you the word of God in its fullness—the mystery that has been kept hidden for ages and generations, but is now disclosed to the saints. To them God has chosen to make known among the Gentiles the glorious riches of this mystery, which is Christ in you, the hope of glory."
- ◆ 2nd Timothy 3:16
    - o "All Scripture is God-breathed and is useful for teaching, rebuking, correcting and training in righteousness"

- Genesis 3:23
    - "So the LORD God banished him from the Garden of Eden to work the ground from which he had been taken."
- Hebrews 7:26
    - "Such a high priest meets our need—one who is holy, blameless, pure, set apart from sinners, exalted above the heavens."
- Romans 6:23
    - "For the wages of sin is death, but the gift of God is eternal life in Christ Jesus our Lord."
- Genesis 6:11–14
    - "Now the earth was corrupt in God's sight and was full of violence. God saw how corrupt the earth had become, for all the people on earth had cor-

rupted their ways. So God said to Noah, "I am going to put an end to all people, for the earth is filled with violence because of them. I am surely going to destroy both them and the earth. So make yourself an ark of cypress wood; make rooms in it and coat it with pitch inside and out."

- Genesis Chapter 5/from Adam to Noah
  - "This is the written account of Adam's line. When God created man, he made him in the likeness of God. He created them male and female and blessed them. And when they were created, he called them "man". When Adam had lived 130 years, he had a son in his

own likeness, in his own image; and he named him Seth. After Seth was born, Adam lived 800 years and had other sons and daughters. Altogether, Adam lived 930 years, and then he died. When Seth had lived 105 years, he became the father of Enosh. And after he became the father of Enosh, Seth lived 807 years and had other sons and daughters. Altogether, Seth lived 912 years, and then he died. When Enosh had lived 90 years, he became the father of Kenan. And after he became the father of Kenan, Enosh lived 815 years and had other sons and daughters. Altogether, Enosh lived 905 years, and then he died. When

Kenan had lived 70 years, he became the father of Mahalalel. And after he became the father of Mahalalel, Kenan lived 840 years and had other sons and daughters. Altogether, Kenan lived 910 years, and then he died. When Mahalalel had lived 65 years, he became the father of Jared. And after he became the father of Jared, Mahalalel lived 830 years and had other sons and daughters. Altogether, Mahalalel lived 895 years, and then he died. When Jared had lived 162 years, he became the father of Enoch. And after he became the father of Enoch, Jared lived 800 years and had other sons and daughters. Altogether,

Jared lived 962 years, and then he died. When Enoch had lived 65 years, he became the father of Methuselah. And after he became the father of Methuselah, Enoch walked with God 300 years and had other sons and daughters. Altogether, Enoch lived 365 years. Enoch walked with God; then he was no more, because God took him away. When Methuselah had lived 187 years, he became the father of Lamech. And after he became the father of Lamech, Methuselah lived 782 years and had other sons and daughters. Altogether, Methuselah lived 969 years, and then he died. When Lamech had lived

182 years, he had a son. He named him Noah and said, "He will comfort us in the labor and painful toil of our hands caused by the ground the LORD has cursed." After Noah was born, Lamech lived 595 years and had other sons and daughters. Altogether, Lamech lived 777 years, and then he died. After Noah was 500 years old, he became the father of Shem, Ham and Japheth."

- 2nd Peter 3:9
  - "The Lord is not slow in keeping his promise, as some understand slowness. He is patient with you, not wanting anyone to perish, but everyone to come to repentance."

- Romans 3:10–12
    - As it is written: "There is no one righteous, not even one; there is no one who understands, no one who seeks God. All have turned away, they have together become worthless; there is no one who does good, not even one."
- John 1:1–3
    - "In the beginning was the Word, and the Word was with God, and the Word was God. He was with God in the beginning. Through him all things were made; without him nothing was made that has been made."
- John 14:6
    - Jesus answered, "I am the way and the truth and the life. No

one comes to the Father except through me."

- John 1:29
  - The next day John saw Jesus coming toward him and said, "Look, the Lamb of God, who takes away the sin of the world!"
- John 14:16–17
  - And I will ask the Father, and he will give you another Counselor to be with you forever—the Spirit of truth. The world cannot accept him, because it neither sees him nor knows him. But you know him, for he lives with you and will be in you.
- Mathew 11:28–30
  - "Come to me, all you who are weary and burdened, and I will

give you rest. Take my yoke upon you and learn from me, for I am gentle and humble in heart, and you will find rest for your souls. For my yoke is easy and my burden is light."

- Matthew 7:24–27
  - "Therefore everyone who hears these words of mine and puts them into practice is like a wise man who built his house on the rock. The rain came down, the streams rose, and the winds blew and beat against that house; yet it did not fall, because it had its foundation on the rock. But everyone who hears these words of mine and does not put them into practice is like a foolish man who built his house on sand. The

When I Come Up Missing

rain came down, the streams rose, and the winds blew and beat against that house, and it fell with a great crash."

- Acts 9:1–9
  - Meanwhile, Saul was still breathing out murderous threats against the Lord's disciples. He went to the high priest and asked him for letters to the synagogues in Damascus, so that if he found any there who belonged to the Way, whether men or women, he might take them as prisoners to Jerusalem. As he neared Damascus on his journey, suddenly a light from heaven flashed around him. He fell to the ground and heard a voice say to him, "Saul, Saul, why

do you persecute me?" "Who are you, Lord?" Saul asked. "I am Jesus, whom you are persecuting," he replied. "Now get up and go into the city, and you will be told what you must do." The men traveling with Saul stood there speechless; they heard the sound but did not see anyone. Saul got up from the ground, but when he opened his eyes he could see nothing. So they led him by the hand into Damascus. For three days he was blind, and did not eat or drink anything.

- Matthew 7:12
  - So in everything, do to others what you would have them do to you, for this sums up the Law and the Prophets.

- Deuteronomy 6:1–9
  - These are the commands, decrees and laws the Lord your God directed me to teach you to observe in the land that you are crossing the Jordan to possess, so that you, your children and their children after them may fear the Lord your God as long as you live by keeping all his decrees and commands that I give you, and so that you may enjoy long life. Hear, O Israel: The Lord our God, the Lord is one. Love the Lord your God with all your heart and with all your soul and with all your strength. These commandments that I give you today are to be upon your hearts. Impress them on

your children. Talk about them when you sit at home and when you walk along the road, when you lie down and when you get up. Tie them as symbols on your hands and bind them on your foreheads. Write them on the doorframes of your houses and on your gates.

- Romans 1:18–2:9
  - The wrath of God is being revealed from heaven against all the godlessness and wickedness of men who suppress the truth by their wickedness, since what may be known about God is plain to them, because God has made it plain to them. For since the creation of the world God's invisible qualities—his eternal power

and divine nature—have been clearly seen, being understood from what has been made, so that men are without excuse. For although they knew God, they neither glorified him as God nor gave thanks to him, but their thinking became futile and their foolish hearts were darkened. Although they claimed to be wise, they became fools and exchanged the glory of the immortal God for images made to look like mortal man and birds and animals and reptiles. Therefore God gave them over in the sinful desires of their hearts to sexual impurity for the degrading of their bodies with one another. They exchanged the truth of God for a lie, and worshiped and served created things rather than the Creator—who is forever praised. Amen. Because of this, God gave them over to shameful lusts. Even their women exchanged natural relations for unnatural ones. In the same way the men also abandoned natural relations with women and were inflamed with lust for one another. Men committed indecent acts with other men, and received in themselves the due penalty for their perversion. Furthermore, since they did not think it worthwhile to retain the knowledge of God, he gave them over to a depraved mind, to do what ought not to be done. They have become filled with every kind of wickedness, evil, greed and depravity. They are full of envy, murder, strife, deceit and malice. They are gossips, slanderers, God-haters, insolent, arrogant and boastful; they invent ways of doing evil; they disobey their parents; they are senseless, faithless, heartless, ruthless. Although they know God's righteous decree that those who do such things deserve death, they not only continue to do these very things but also approve of those who practice them.

- James 2:19
  - You believe that there is one God. Good! Even the demons believe that—and shudder.

Question and Answer Session

Q: How can I trust the Bible since it has been revised so many times?

A: This is a very common question and a valid one at that. The 66 books that comprise the Bible were written in a number of stages. The OT (Old Testament) was written over the course of approximately 900 years before Christ. When the Dead Sea Scrolls were found in the late 1940s to early 1950s, original text from the earliest Hebrew Bible was discovered. This adds much credibility to the translations that we have available today. Each translation made over the past number of centuries has been made

When I Come Up Missing

from the original texts rather than from one to the next to the next. The NT (New Testament) was authored during the late first century and the Bible was considered complete around the mid to late fourth century. These books were originally written primarily in Greek and Hebrew. The best know translation in English is the King James Version (KJV) and that was written in the early 1600s. Because a number of the words in the original languages are not completely translatable into English words, there was liberty taken to explain what was meant in the original text. Since the KJV is still a little difficult to understand compared to modern English, there have been additional more "easy to read" versions made available. The NKJV (New King James Version), NIV (New International Version), NASB (New American Standard Bible) and NLT (New Living Translation) just to name a few, have been revised so the reader can establish a better picture in their head of the times and events of the day. Even though you may pick up three different versions and they may not read word for word, the lesson will be the same. If not, then you need to question the version that you are reading. Unfortunately there are some Bibles being produced these days that are considered politically correct and that isn't how Jesus taught. Steer clear of these types of versions. I have included a sample verse from three different versions so that you can see the difference.

Matthew 6:34

- ♦ KJV: Take therefore no thought for the morrow: for the morrow shall take thought for the things of itself. Sufficient unto the day is the evil thereof.

- NASB: Therefore do not be anxious for tomorrow; for tomorrow will care for itself. Each day has enough trouble of its own.
- NLT: So don't worry about tomorrow, for tomorrow will bring its own worries. Today's trouble is enough for today.

Q: Why do "good" people go to hell?

A: Another legitimate and commonly asked question. The answer is simple. No one is good enough on their own to go to heaven. Even people who appear good to us are not perfect and perfection is required by God to be in His presence. That is exactly why He sent Jesus to die on the cross for our sins; it is through the perfection of Jesus that we are allowed in to heaven. The requirement is to believe that this is true! If "good" people don't trust in Jesus' perfection instead of their own, they will not enter the Kingdom of Heaven.

Q: But I don't want God to control my life!
A: OK this isn't a question but rather a statement. It is true though, am I right?
I would suggest that you just start small. Don't picture Him running your life or think about all of the things that you assume He will want you to quit doing. Give serious thought to your current struggles and trials. Are you in a spot where you really want a better life, a better marriage, the ability to pay your bills each month and some plain old peace? I know from experience that the only way to reach these goals is with our Heavenly Father's help, which He gladly gives. As you see Him change you and cause things in your life to improve, you will no longer think about the things that brought you fear over giving Him con-

trol. As you experience the joy of knowing God in a very personal way, you will gladly look to Him for advice and help because He is really good at it!

Q: Why should I believe all of this is going to happen?
A: Most people would think that odds of 60–70% would be good if you are gambling or playing the stock market. As those numbers increase, then you become even more encouraged to take a risk. Well, what if the odds were 100%? That is a sure thing... guaranteed! Highly unlikely though, right? God gave us over 2500 prophecies in the Bible and over 2000 have already come to pass with absolute 100% accuracy. History proves this fact. The remaining prophecies are future to you and me but guaranteed to happen given God's track record.

For the following questions, I haven't provided answers because I want you to seek them from the person who gave you this book or search them out yourself.

- Q: Where do I begin?
- Q: Do I have to go to church?
- Q: Why is there so much war and fighting over religion?
- Q: Why was there so much killing in the OT?
- Q: What does Israel have to do with anything?
- Q: What is baptism?
- Q: Is Jesus really the only way to heaven? What about all of the other religions out there?
- Q: What if my sin is too great to be forgiven?
- Q: Will I have to quit smoking, drinking, living with my girlfriend/boyfriend?

- Q: What about the family members who won't be happy with my decision?
- Q: Can you prove Jesus' resurrection?

Biblically Sound Authors

Oswald Chambers, *My Utmost for His Highest*
Dr. David Jeremiah, *What in the World is Going On?*
(This book pertains to Bible Prophesy)
Max Lucado, *Experiencing the Words of Jesus*
John MacArther, *The Gospel According to Jesus*
Chuck Smith, *Living Water*
Charles Stanley, *In Step With God*
Charles Swindoll, *The Owner's Manual for Christians*

Solid Christian Websites

DavidJeremiah.org
focusonthefamily.com
twft.com
joncourson.com
loveworthfinding.org
moodyministries.net

The authors and websites listed above are superb. However, there are many other wonderful teachers who are biblically correct. Not all information out there *is* accurate, so be cautious whose material you choose.